How To Stay Away From Lust One Day At A Time

New Thought and Sex Addicts

VOLUME ONE

by

EDWARD L.

Emmet L. Billroy Publishers, Inc.

ISBN: 1-890316-00-8

This edition is printed in the United States of America by Bookcrafters

THE FIRST BOOK OF MOSES, called **GENESIS.**

1 In the beginning God created the heaven and the earth.

2 And the earth was without form, and void; and darkness was upon the face of the deep. And the Spirit of God moved upon the face of the waters.

3 And God said, "Let there be light:" and there was light.

4 And God saw the light, that it was good: and God divided the light from the darkness.

5 And God called the light Day, and the darkness He called Night. And the evening and the morning were the first day.

6 And God said, "Let there be a firmament in the midst of the waters, and let it divide the waters from the waters."

7 And God made the firmament, and divided the waters which were under the firmament from the waters which were above the firmament: and it was so.

8 And God called the firmament Heaven. And the evening and the morning were the second day.

9 And God said, "Let the waters under the heaven be gathered together unto one place, and let the dry land appear:" and it was so.

10 And God called the dry land Earth; and the gathering together of the waters called He Seas: and God saw that it was good.

11 And God said, "Let the earth bring forth grass, the herb yielding seed, and the fruit tree yielding fruit after his kind, whose seed is in itself, upon the earth:" and it was so.

12 And the earth brought forth grass, and herb yielding seed after his kind, and the tree yielding fruit, whose seed was in itself, after his kind: and God saw that it was good.

13 And the evening and the morning were the third day.

14 And God said, "Let there be lights in the firmament of the heaven to divide the day from the night; and let them be for signs, and for seasons, and for days, and years:

15 And let them be for lights in the firmament of the heaven to give light upon the earth:" and it was so.

16 And God made two great lights; the greater light to rule the day, and the lesser light to rule the night: He made the stars also.

17 And God set them in the firmament of the heaven to give light upon the earth.

18 And to rule over the day and over the night, and to divide the light from the darkness: and God saw that it was good.

19 And the evening and the morning were the fourth day.

20 And God said, "Let the waters bring forth abundantly the moving creature that hath life, and fowl that may fly above the earth in the open firmament of heaven."

21 And God created great whales, and every living creature that moveth, which the waters brought forth abundantly, after their kind, and every winged fowl, after his kind: and God saw that it was good.

22 And God blessed them, saying, "Be fruitful, and multiply, and fill the waters in the seas, and let fowl multiply in the earth."

23 And the evening and the morning were the fifth day.

24 And God said, "Let the earth bring forth the living creature after his kind, cattle, and creeping thing, and beast of the earth after his kind:" and it was so.

25 And God made the beast of the earth after his kind, and cattle after their kind, and every thing that creepeth upon the earth after his kind: and God saw that it was good.

26 And God said, "Let Us make man in Our image, after Our likeness: and let them have dominion over the fish of the sea, and over the fowl of the air, and over the cattle, and over all the earth, and over every creeping thing that creepeth upon the earth."

27 So God created man in His own image, in the image of God created He him; male and female created He them.

28 And God blessed them, and God said unto them, "Be fruitful, and multiply, and replenish the earth, and subdue it: and have dominion over the fish of the sea, and over the fowl of the air, and over every living thing that moveth upon the earth."

29 And God said, "Behold, I have given you every herb bearing seed, which is upon the face of all the earth, and every tree, in the which is the fruit of a tree yielding seed; to you it shall be for meat.

30 And to every beast of the earth, and to every fowl of the air, and to every thing that creepeth upon the earth, wherein there is life, I have given every green herb for meat:" and it was so.

31 And God saw every thing that He had made, and behold, it was very good. And the evening and the morning were the sixth day.

THE TWELVE STEPS OF ALCOHOLICS ANONYMOUS

1. We admitted we were powerless over alcohol - that our lives had become unmanageable.

2. Came to believe that a Power greater than ourselves could restore us to sanity.

3. Made a decision to turn our will and our lives over to the care of God *as we understood Him.*

4. Made a searching and fearless moral inventory of ourselves.

5. Admitted to God, to ourselves and to another human being the exact nature of our wrongs.

6. Were entirely ready to have God remove all these defects of character.

7. Humbly ask Him to remove our shortcomings.

8. Made a list of all persons we had harmed, and became willing to make amends to them all.

9. Made direct amends to such people wherever possible, except when to do so would injure them or others.

10. Continued to take personal inventory and when we were wrong promptly admitted it.

11. Sought through prayer and meditation to improve our conscious contact with God, *as we understood Him,* praying only for knowledge of His will for us and the power to carry that out.

12. Having had a spiritual awakening as the result of these steps, we tried to carry this message to alcoholics, and to practice these principles in all our affairs.

In the beginning God created the heaven and the earth.
GENESIS 1:1

T here has never been a beginning because you and I have always existed in the Mind of God. You and I were never born and we will never die. That is the Good News. And since you and I were made in the image and likeness of God, and we partake of the very nature of God, we can also create, just like God creates. We create the thoughts that set in motion their own consequences, or manifestations, in the outer universe that we see all around us. Our lives are the reflections of our thoughts. All of our circumstances, our happiness, our harmony, health, success, and prosperity are all the outer manifestation of our own thoughts. Similarly, any seeming unhappiness, disharmony, sickness, failure, and poverty are, likewise, the consequences of our own negative thinking. For God has given us free will to choose between Truth and error. For instance, if we are untreated lust addicts, and if we deliberately engage in the practice of lust fantasies or various forms of sexual acting-out behavior, we shall reap the whirlwind of such behavior in our outer circumstances as well as our inner feelings: misery, conflicts, sickness and disease, failure, poverty, depression, remorse, guilt, fear, resentment, etc...Ask any sexaholic who has just "slipped" by masturbating how he feels immediately after sexually acting out. He will tell you: Guilt, remorse, and depression all assail him mercilessly.

This is the Law of Cause and Effect. It has been known since the beginning of history. And it is one of the most important Laws illustrated in the Bible. We shall see countless examples of it as we read through the Bible in this book of Bible interpretation. In this series of volumes, we will read every verse of the Bible in the Book of Genesis. We shall see how it may be interpreted according to the laws of metaphysics, and how it illustrates the problems surrounding lust and sexual addiction. At this stage of the human race we are experiencing an epidemic of lust and the Bible has much to teach us in this regard.

And the earth was without form and void; and darkness was upon the face of the deep.
And the Spirit of God moved upon the face of the waters.

GENESIS 1:2

The "earth," of course, in metaphysics or scientific Christianity stands for outward manifestation, which is the result of our thinking. If our outer life (work, friends, activities, prosperity etc...) is "without form and void," it is generally because our thinking has been full of negativity, such as fear, resentment, or lust, and, indeed, it can be truly said that that "darkness" is upon the face of our "deep," which means our human soul. In order to be restored to sanity, the "Spirit of God" needs to move upon the face of our human soul. Now in the Bible, water frequently symbolizes the human soul. So when the Spirit of God moves upon the face of our soul, we are, indeed, restored to sanity. But the Spirit of God must move upon the face of our soul in order for this to happen, and it will only happen if we humbly ask Him.

And God said, "Let there be light:" and there was light.
GENESIS 1:3

L ight, of course, symbolizes Truth. In order to "see the light" about any matter, God has to speak to us. In order to have this take place, we need to be in intimate communication with God, which takes place during prayer and meditation. Prayer and meditation is thinking about God. Negative emotions, such as fear, resentment, or lust, have no place in prayer and meditation. However, because lust differs from fear and resentment in that the former is pleasurable to a sexaholic, whereas the latter are experienced as being distinctly unpleasant, it is possible for the lust addict to try to use prayer and meditation to obtain the lust that he covets. In other words, he misuses the power of Spirit to help him or her to achieve the unhealthy union that he covets. And, since the Principles of Mind action are impersonal, and work the same way for whomever uses them, he or she may temporarily achieve some of the error desires that he or she covets, just as a thief or a liar may have some temporary successes in the beginning. This, of course is truly a form of satanism, or the use of spiritual laws to achieve ignoble ends. Whoever tries this will reap misery in the long run.

And God saw the light, that it was good: and God divided the
light from the darkness.

GENESIS 1:4

L ight, as we saw earlier, stands for Truth. Conversely, darkness, symbolizes error. Now error does not exist in Truth, which means that it *does not exist.* This is the greatest lesson that scientific Christianity teaches: There is nothing but Good. Good is a synonym for God. Therefore, we are all ideas in the Mind of God. Seeming evil in the world is only the result of man's free will choosing error, because of ignorance or stupidity. But as an inevitable result of trial and error, man discovers that there is a difference between Truth and error. Truth and error produce different consequences. Truth produces happiness, harmony, health, success, and prosperity. Error causes sin, sickness, and death. People who are addicted to something: alcohol, drugs, overeating, gambling, shoplifting, lust etc.... are the luckiest people in the world, actually, because the *consequences* for them are so much more devastating and acute than for "normal" people. "Normal" people can get away with getting drunk or high once in a while, or binging on food, "social" gambling, or "social" lusting without experiencing the devastation that this same activity will produce in an addict. One drink, and the alcoholic is off and running again, and it may all end up in the cemetery quickly. The social drinker, on the other hand, can drink moderately and even, at times, excessively, without devastating consequences. Similarly, the "social" luster can get away, seemingly, with occasional lust thoughts in his heart, or coveting his neighbor's wife, or leafing through the "Swimsuit Issue" of *Sports Illustrated*, or occasionally masturbating, whereas the sexaholic who relapses may lose his reputation in the community when he is arrested for propositioning an undercover policewoman, or, worse, catching the HIV virus by engaging in unprotected sex with an infected partner. Therefore, since the consequences for an addict are usually so much more destructive than for the "normal" person, he or she is really the lucky one, because the pain of practicing his addiction becomes a motive for seeking help, and, in the recovery process, he or she learns about the difference between Truth and error. His or her life then depends upon learning that difference. As a result, most recovering addicts become deeply spiritual people. Not necessarily religious (although this may happen also), but spiritual. They have been through the wringer. They become willing as only the dying can be. A deeply spiritual person who is not an addict may also learn about the difference between Truth and error, sometimes by trial and error, because he or she may become more sensitive to the deleterious effect of error thoughts, and the correspondingly beneficial effects of Truth thoughts in his or her life.

The "light" stands for Truth, as mentioned before, and darkness stands for error. Since evil, as an entity, does not really exist, we simply call it "error." But there is a difference between Truth and error, and that is the great lesson of verse four. We already know there is a difference between Truth and error, because practicing either one brings about very different consequences on the earthly plane. Some people sometimes try to tell us that there is no difference between Truth and error, and that these are only opinions, but this is not so. There **IS** a difference between Truth and error. Truth brings about happiness, harmony, health, success, and prosperity. Error brings about sin, sickness, and death. "God <u>divided</u> the light from the darkness," because they are different. Dividing the light from the darkness is God's way of telling us that they are different. However, it is not always easy to tell the difference. That is one of the purposes of living: To learn that difference. Knowing the difference between the Truth and error of any given situation is called <u>discrimination</u>. Discrimination is being able to distinguish between things. For instance, being able to distinguish between a good movie and a bad movie, a good book and a bad book, a good poem and a bad poem, would be artistic discrimination. A musician knows the difference between good singing and bad singing. An engineer, if he is provided with the pertinent information, can tell the difference between a bridge that will stand up and one that will fall down under certain conditions. Most of us can tell when there are "good vibes" or "bad vibes" about a certain individual we meet for the first time. A gourmet can tell the difference between a good souffle and a bad souffle. The terms "good" and "bad" here do not necessarily connote moral qualities, they are merely descriptive of situations we commonly encounter. The kind of discrimination I am talking about here is the discrimination that determines the Truth or error of any given situation for any given individual. For instance, a recovering alcoholic knows that if he picks up a drink, it will probably entail a series of consequences, very unpleasant in their nature, which may lead to loss of job, loss of marriage, loss of health, and maybe loss of life. Therefore, for him, to pick up that drink would constitute "error," and not picking up that drink would constitute Truth. Similarly, for a recovering sexaholic, to voluntarily lust in his heart about any particular lust object might probably lead to acting out sexually, either by masturbation or having sex with another person, which would bring as immediate consequences remorse, depression, and guilt, and further compulsive behavior along the same lines, which might, in turn, entail marital strife (if he were married), loss of ability to function in the work place, financial problems, suicidal tendencies, HIV infection, loss of standing in the community, and/or death. Therefore, for him, voluntarily lusting in his heart would constitute "error," whereas the maintenance of sexual sobriety in his heart would constitute Truth. For a "normal" person (i.e., a non-addicted person), the Truth or error of any particular situation might be less "black-and-white," but, nevertheless, clear, depending upon that person's psychological or spiritual development. For instance, a normal person is tempted by the offer of a piece a chocolate cake at dinner. He reasons that because he is overweight, he needs to abstain from concentrated sweets. Therefore, for him, declining the cake would be Truth, and eating the cake would be error, and so forth and so on. If the man or woman involved were a diabetic, but otherwise "normal" (i.e., non-addicted), the error or Truth involved would be even more "black-and-white," than if he or she were merely on a weight reduction diet.

Now there is a difference between <u>discrimination</u> and <u>criticism</u>. The second involves personal judgment that somebody is "bad" and deserves to be condemned because he or she is behaving a certain way or has done certain things. <u>Discrimination</u> involves the "sin," and <u>criticism</u> involves the "sinner," so to speak. In the interpretation of this part of the Bible, we are dealing with discrimination rather than criticism, right at the moment, but there will be other times and/or passages where we will discuss criticism. Both are important concepts, and the difference between them is also important.

*And God called the light Day, and darkness He called Night.
And the evening and morning were the first day.*

GENESIS 1:5

T his verse amplifies what we have been talking about. In the Bible, "day" symbolizes Truth, and night "error." The "first day" symbolizes the beginning of spiritual development. In my case, my spiritual development began when I admitted that I was powerless over alcohol and that my life had become unmanageable, and turned my will and my life over to the care of Alcoholics Anonymous on June 4, 1978. My whole attitude on life began to change. That was the first day of my new life.

And God said, "Let there be a firmament in the midst of the waters, and let it divide the waters from the waters."

GENESIS 1:6

ebster defines firmament as "the sky or heavens, viewed poetically as a solid arch or vault." The waters above the firmament symbolize error, and the waters below the firmament symbolize Truth. This is further evidence that God wants us to discriminate between Truth and error. Otherwise He would not have created a firmament to divide them. Now we know, of course, that there is no such thing as a firmament in the sky the way the ancients conceived it. It was just their way of conceptualizing the universe. The ancients literally felt that the stars and planets were placed in the firmament. The Bible is not always to be taken literally, or we do a great disservice to common sense. God does not want us to violate our common sense in order to worship Him. But if we begin to see that the firmament really means an established foundation or basis for our understanding of the universe, we begin to comprehend the spiritual meaning of this verse. It means our faith and understanding about the Truth. Whatever we have faith in or understand will come true for us, and is, therfore, underneath our firmament. It will come into manifestation. Our lack of faith and understanding about the Truth will not come true for us, because it is beyond our firmament. These are the waters of negativity or error. They do not exist in Truth. For the sexaholic, lust falls into this category, and the sexaholic who tries to practice lust is trying to reach for the waters beyond the firmament. If he practices lust, he will lose faith and understanding, and, eventually lose control over his own life and mind. He will lose both his life and his mind, in this world and the world to come.

And God made the firmament, and divided the waters which were under the firmament from the waters which were above the firmament: and it was so.

GENESIS 1:7

his is just more repetition for the sake of poetry and emphasis, which eastern writers like to use. The inspired writer of this passage was from the east, and the eastern mode of expression likes to use this type of rhythmical, concentrated reiteration for the sake of better impressing it upon the soul of the listener or reader. In this book we use the King James translation of the Bible, which is the most beautiful and poetic version of the Bible that we have in English. The last four words, "and it was so" refer to the fact that reality in our world of manifestation always reflects Principle. Principle refers to the Law of Cause and Effect. There are no mistakes in God's world. We reap what we sow. The Law of Compensation, as Emerson said, never fails. There is no such thing as "bad things" happening to good people. In the scheme of God's universe, seemingly bad things sometimes happen to seemingly good people, but things are never what they seem. There is the appearance, and then there is the reality. One of my ministers used to say, when something seemingly unpleasant happened, "I can hardly wait to see the good that will come out of this." I myself can now look upon some past incidents in my life, such as the divorce from my third wife, and see that, unpleasant-seeming as it was at the time, in retrospect, now, five years later, it was one of the best things that ever happened to me. It led to my learning to stand on my own two feet, and to learn that sex is, indeed, optional.

And God called the firmament Heaven. And the evening and the morning were the second day.

GENESIS 1:8

ow we have learned that "firmament" means faith. "Heaven" also has a spiritual meaning. Heaven is not a physical place beyond the sky. Heaven is right here, right now. Heaven is the consciousness of the Presence of God. Evening symbolizes darkness or error, and Morning symbolizes light or Truth. The second day does not mean the second "twenty four hours," it means the second period of unfoldment in the consciousness of man or woman. For the sexaholic man or woman, it means that "evening" includes lust, fear, and resentment, and all the other character defects that he or she has uncovered by doing a "fourth Step" inventory. "Morning" includes assets, such as sexual sobriety, faith, perseverance, fortitude, Love etc...The process of growing up in sobriety involves Steps six and seven: "Were entirely ready to have God remove all these defects of character" and "Humbly asked Him remove our shortcomings." As the character defects are removed, assets come in to take their place easily and effortlessly. This process takes place almost automatically in the sober recovering sexaholic, as a function of time in the Program spent working the Steps.

And God said, "Let the waters under the heaven be gathered together unto one place, and let the dry land appear:" and it was so.

GENESIS 1:9

T he "waters under the heaven" in this verse have reference to the consciousness of Truth that we have developed in our minds. And the "dry land" refers to the outward manifestation of this consciousness of Truth. Another word for outward manifestation is "demonstration." When we pray for something, and <u>know</u> that the prayer is being answered, right here and right now, then we have the "consciousness of Truth" in our minds. When the prayer has been answered in the outer world, for all to see, then we have had a "demonstration." When "..Jesus lifted up *his* eyes, and said, 'Father, I thank Thee that Thou hast heard Me,[1]'" he was experiencing a consciousness of Truth in his own Mind. But when Lazarus "..that was dead came forth, bound hand and foot with graveclothes.."[2] the prayer was answered in the outer world, for all to see. This second event was the demonstration. "And it was so" reiterates the Law of Cause and Effect: As above, so below. As in heaven, so on earth. As the Father, so the Son. Whatever we pray for, believing that we have received it, and thanking God <u>ahead of time</u> will be

---

[1]John 11:41
[2]John 11:44

demonstrated, if we have risen high enough in consciousness. If we pray for sexual sobriety on our knees before going to bed, remaining long enough in prayer to raise our consciousness sufficiently, we will be spared the expression of lust known as "wet dreams" during the night. This never fails. Sometimes, I am too tired to continue in prayer until the conclusion of my prayer. Sometimes I pray too fast or with insufficient concentration. In those cases I may become subject to lust temptations during sleep. Especially, these may happen when I do not pray at all, as occasionally happens. But these occurrences do not indicate a failure of the Law. They reveal the failure of my state of consciousness.

When I concentrate the mind on one particular problem or the solution to that problem through prayer or treatment, the "waters under the heaven" are being "gathered together unto one place." "Waters" in this case symbolizes ideas of divine Mind, which I am going over in my own mind, such as Love, Truth, Intelligence, Spirit etc...Since the "real me" is an individualization of God, just as sparks are an individualization of fire, I can think the same thoughts that God thinks. And when I think Godly thoughts about any particular situation, the situation is resolved, if I have sufficient faith and gratitude. This is prayer or treatment. To apply this to sexual addiction, this means, if I am tempted by lust, say, by a particular lust object or fantasy, then if I wish to maintain my sexual sobriety, my first duty is to admit my powerlessness and to pray for God's power to take it away. This is the first Step of Alcoholics Anonymous: "We admitted we were powerless over alcohol—that our lives had become unmanageable." The word "alcohol" of course, may be substituted by "lust." This admission of unmanageability means that "of myself I am nothing." My own limited self has no power over lust, because I am truly addicted to it. But when God's power is substituted for my power, then lust may be overcome. Another way of putting this is: "God, I am powerless. Help me." Now a standard treatment that I use is to repeat the following to myself slowly aloud or silently:

> 1. A fixed certainty that every need will be met easily, without difficulty.
> 2. Treat the treatment. (If I have already prayed that day to have lust removed, and if I do not want to repeat the treatment twice, because it may indicate a lack of faith in the first treatment, I 'treat the treatment.')
> 3. I do not accept your negative thoughts, feelings, or images of me. I send these back to you. If you do not accept them back, they go into the healing substance all around to be dissolved into the nothingness that it is. (I use this formula if a live, human lust object is involved, who may be subconsciously participating in the lust.)
> 4. God bless her (him, it, etc. "Her," "him," or "it" refers to the lust object or fantasy involved).
> 5. Thank you, God, for telling me how much I love you. Thank you, God for this victory over lust. Thank you, God, for the joy response.
> 6. Thank you, God, for this demonstration.
> 7. I release this treatment and let it go.

If a fantasy is involved rather than a live lust object, then I change no. 3 as follows: "The sword of the Lord and of Gideon!" to indicate Denial of the error thought.

Repeating this or a similar treatment never fails to take the temptation away, at least temporarily. I may have to do it all over again five minutes or one hour later. One of the best brief treatments is to use "Jesus Christ" as a mantra, and repeat it over and over when assailed severely by temptation, either of the lust variety, or some other type of temptation, such as resentment or fear. If you are not a Christian, there are other mantras that you can use. The "dry land" refers to the demonstration that results from a successful prayer or treatment. In the case of the sexaholic, "dry land" would refer to the elimination of the lust temptation, even temporarily, from his mind. As stated above, the temptation may recur, in which case another treatment is required, if one wishes to maintain sobriety. In early sobriety (i.e., the first year of sobriety), it is not uncommon for a sexaholic to have one hundred or more lust temptations in one day. After several years of continuous sexual sobriety, the frequency of these "lust attacks" may decrease to once every two or three weeks. However, one should not be deceived. The sexaholic is just as powerless each time the lust attack presents itself, no matter how long he has been sober. At the time of the lust attack, he is just as powerless as any newcomer. But unlike the newcomer, he probably has more tools in his kit box for dealing with it. But, like the newcomer, if he fails to ask God to have the temptation removed, he will act out sooner or later. And if he acts out, he will soon experience a pitiful and incomprehensible demoralization as the addiction resumes its course, relentlessly careening to the edge of the falls. Then, as the sexaholic goes over the edge, he may unaccountably find himself separated or divorced, incarcerated, hospitalized, or even dead. This disease is, indeed, cunning, baffling, and powerful, and should never be underestimated. "And it was so," of course, refers to the inevitability of the operation of these principles, which stands for the Law of Cause and effect. This law is impersonal, just as the law of gravity is impersonal. It does not matter if a very important man falls out of a tenth story window, he will still come crashing to the earth, just as much as "Joe Blow" will. If we practice lust, we will reap the consequences.

And God called the dry land Earth; and the gathering together of the waters called He Seas: and God saw that it was good.

GENESIS 1:10

arth symbolizes manifestation in the outer or formed world. "Gathering together" refers to concentration, and "waters" mental potentiality. "Seas" means universal Mind. This is a reiteration of the fact that the outer, formed world is but a reflection of universal Mind. Since each one of us is an individualization of God, we can, by concentrating our own thoughts in prayer or treatment, change our own outer conditions: Our health, happiness, harmony, success, and prosperity. Every situation in our life can be changed. This can be done through the power of thought. This is a principle of scientific Christianity. Principle is one of the most important facets of God. Since it is an aspect of God, it is "good." Now this principle of the power of thought can also be used for ill. If a man or woman spends his or her time thinking or fantasizing about lust, then he or she is using his or her power of thought to concentrate on error. What will the result of this be in his or her outer world? The answer to this question is very simple: sickness, unhappiness, disharmony, failure, and poverty. A short-handed way of putting it, using only three words, is: Sin, sickness, and death.

*And God said, "Let the earth bring forth grass, the herb
yielding seed, and the fruit tree yielding fruit after his kind,
whose seed is in itself, upon the earth:" and it was so.*

GENESIS 1:11

T o paraphrase this verse of the Bible, the inspired writer is saying that each form of vegetation upon the earth is brought forth by its
own cause. The seed brings forth the grass, and the seed
inside the fruit brings forth the fruit tree itself. In other
words, each kind of vegetation can only be brought forth
by its own specific antecedent. The herb seed cannot
bring forth a fruit tree, and the seed inside the fruit cannot
bring forth grass. Each cause has its own specific effect.
Similarly, when we pray or treat, if we pray for financial
success, we will not necessarily get harmony. If we pray
for sobriety, we will not necessarily obtain happiness
with our wife. In God's world it is necessary to be as
specific as possible when treating or praying. That does
not mean that we outline to God or tell him how to do it.
General prayers, such as, "His will for us and the power
to carry it out" will improve our entire outlook on life and
our general functioning in an overall way, but they will
do it very incrementally. But if we want to "get Mrs.
Jones off our back," we must pray specifically for this:
"God, get Mrs. Jones off my back." But we must also
bless Mrs. Jones and wish her well, because prayers
including anger or resentment are only answered in a
negative way. If we continue to resent Mrs. Jones, we
will probably end up seeing <u>more</u> of her, not less. But if

we forgive Mrs. Jones and wish her well, and, in addition ask God to get her off our back, and if we rise high enough in consciousness while doing this, then our prayer will be successful, and we will find that Mrs. Jones is no longer bothering us after a while. The Bible is written in allegory. This verse is not particularly significant, if all it is talking about is grass and fruit trees. Seed means the source, origin, or beginning of anything (Webster). Now the origin of all manifestation is God, and for anything to be created God must want to have it manifested; therefore, He must make the decision that it is to be manifested. This decision of God is His Word. The seed, consequently, symbolizes the Word, "God said." The seed is creative, just as the Word is creative. And man's word, our word, is also creative within the world of our own conditions. We can bring forth grass and fruit trees in our own world, not literally creating grass or a fruit tree like magic, but creating the grass and fruit trees of our own existence, such as shade, beauty, sustenance for ourselves and our loved ones, through the proper use of the power of our own creative thought.

And the earth brought forth grass, and herb yielding seed after his kind, and the tree yielding fruit, whose seed was in itself, after his kind: and God saw that it was good.
GENESIS 1:12

This is the story of creation in the world of vegetation, the manifest world that we see. And it is a beautiful thing, because "God saw that it was good". Man also uses creation to reproduce himself, using his seed, called sperm. The creative act is associated with the most intense pleasure known to man (and woman), and usually involves man in intense physical, mental, emotional, and spiritual activity in the course of the creative act. The misuse of this creativity for selfish ends is called lust. Lust is the unforgiveable sin, because it involves all four facets of man: the physical, mental, emotional, and spiritual, and affects the very core of his being, and because it is also the most powerful drug in the universe. By comparison, alcohol or cocaine are small potatoes. It is the most addicitive drug in the universe.

And the evening and the morning were the third day.
                                        GENESIS 1:13

T here are seven stages in creation according to the Bible, symbolized by the seven days. Similarly, in any metaphysical treatment or prayer, there are also seven stages. They are as follows: 1) Statement of the Truth of Being; 2) Denial of error; 3) Affirmation of Good; 4) Faith; 5) Gratitude *ahead of time*; 6) Release; 7) Sign or demonstration. The third day is the day of affirmation. We have already learned that evening stands for error, and morning for Truth. You will notice that the words "evening" and "morning" always come in that precise order in this Bible account, with the evening coming first and morning second. Now this inverses the normal order of a day in which evening follows morning. Why? Since "evening" symbolizes error, and error does not exist in Truth, then error does not exist, period. That means that evening does not exist, it is only a handy symbol for something that has no value, like a zero in mathematics. It is, however, an important symbol, in a negative way, because man must learn to distinguish between it and Truth. Evening does not really mean the second part of the twenty four hours, it means error. And since the Bible is really a textbook of meta-physics, we may safely exclude it from the *reality* of the third day. The third day is a day of Affirmation, a day that proclaims, "There is nothing but Good."

And God said, "Let there be lights in the firmament of the heaven to divide the day from the night; and let them be for signs, and for seasons, and for days, and years"
GENESIS 1:14

L ight in the Bible means Understanding. Now Understanding in the metaphysical sense means more than just "comprehension." It also implies Denial. Denial, in New Thought, has a special, technical meaning. It relates to the Second Gate of Revelation in the Bible. It is one of the most important things that we have to do when we perform a Treatment or Prayer. It is the Second Step in Treatment. I will repeat what we discussed earlier in reference to verse 13. The Seven Steps in any Treatment should include: 1) Statement of the Truth of Being; 2) Denial of error; 3) Affirmation of Good; 4) Faith; 5) Gratitude *ahead of time*; 6) Release; 7) Sign or demonstration. So Denial is the Second Step in Treatment. When you are using Denial, you are saying in effect: I do not believe. I do not accept. And you are refusing to believe or accept error. It is very important to get rid of both the subconscious and conscious basis of error in ourselves. By using Denial vehemently, we are not only saying "NO" to the conscious mind in ourselves, we are cleansing the unconscious part of our mind of error. And since, as we have learned, error *does not exist in Truth*, we are in fact doing ourselves an enormous favor by cleansing error out of our system. It is this error that prevents us from becoming what we really want to be, or what God wants us to become. It is what prevents us from demonstrating Happiness, Health, Harmony, Success, and Prosperity in our lives. To the extent that we allow God within us to get rid of the error that still exists in ouselves, to that extent do we grow into the image and likeness of our Creator. To that extent do we allow the Christ within to shine forth. Denial is the Second Step in that process, or in any process of demonstration. Now "firmament," as we noted above, means "faith." So the phrase, "Let there be lights in the firmament" can be translated, metaphysically, as "Let there be Denial accompanying the faith." And this of course means that in order to have a faith that works, we must first use Denial for anything and everything that contradicts that faith. Everything and anything that undermines that faith. In the modern world of today, we have many things that assault our five senses, which seemingly contradict our faith. We are told that sickness is real, that there are diseases that we cannot recover from, so-called "incurable" diseases. We have the worship of modern medicine, and modern "science," to the point of idolatry. We have the veneration of the visible as the only reality. We have the exaltation of death. We have the glorification of self-centered gratification or sensual pleasure as the main goal in life. We have the abandonment of self-discipline as an important tool for right living. We cannot turn the page of a magazine or newspaper without our eyes being assaulted by images of lingerie ads or half-dressed humans. We have books published, with titles such as "Why Bad Things Happen To Good People" that imply that there is no order or causation in the universe, and that chaos is the rule, and that bad things do indeed happen to good people. We have sayings in beer commercials that we only "go around" once in life, that "this" is "all there is," or "this is as good as it gets." And so on and so forth. We have a popular psychology that tells us we are not really living unless we are "feeling our feelings" or "feeling our pain". If we believe that death does not really exist as a reality in our universe, then we are in "denial", according to the "pop psychology" sense of that term.

When the Bible verse says, "Let there be lights in the firmament of the heaven," "of the heaven" of course means "of the mind." Heaven refers to mind, and earth to manifestation. "As in heaven, so on earth". The next phrase, "to divide the day from the night" means, as we indicated above, to separate Truth from error. So the whole sentence so far might be paraphrased, "Let there be Denial accompanying the faith of the mind in order to separate Truth from error". "Signs" means demonstration. "Seasons" means changes, literally, changes in the weather but, symbolically, changes in mental states necessary before a demonstration can take place. "Days" means progression in change, and "years" means more progression in change. It has been said, "The only thing that is constant is change." To live is to change, or alter ourselves, or, better, let God do the job for us if we are willing. Therefore, we could parahrase the entire verse as follows: "And God said, 'Let there be Denial accompanying the faith of the mind in order to separate Truth from error; and let this be for the purpose of Demonstration and for Changes, and for progression of these Changes until there are still greater Changes.'" This paraphrase is obviously quite different from any literal sense of the original. "The letter killeth, but the Spirit giveth Life." To interpret the Bible literally kills the Spirit of the Bible. It reduces the Bible to a husk of its real Self. Its real Self is God speaking to us, to you and me about what God wants us to do in life in order to change and become more like Him.

And let them be for lights in the firmament of the heaven to give light upon the earth:" and it was so.

GENESIS 1:15

N
ow we previously defined firmament as faith and understanding about the Truth. Heaven means the Christ consciousness. It also means the realm of thought generally, just as "earth" refers to manifestation. Now we have said that light meant understanding and also Denial, the Second step in many successful treatments or prayers. Light also stands for Truth, and Truth is one of the Seven Most Important Facets of God. These are: Life, Love, Truth, Intelligence, Soul, Spirit, and Principle. Another "list" consists of the Twelve Gates of the heavenly Jerusalem in Revelation. On these Gates were written the names of the Twelve Tribes, and the foundations of the wall of the city were garnished with precious stones. Each stone corresponds to a Tribe, and each Tribe corresponds to a Gate. These Twelve Gates are as follows: 1) The Name; 2) Denial; 3) Affirmation; 4) Faith; 5) Works; 6) Knowledge; 7) Birth; 8) Sight; 9) Holiness; 10) Forgiveness; 11) Judgement; 12) Praise. There are other metaphysical systems, using mystical numbers such as Seven or Twelve, that classify and explain God's universe. These are "hooks" to hang our concepts on, so that we can more effectively think, pray, treat, love, and live. They are the Lights in the firmament of our Mind that illuminate our Way. We will be examining and discussing these "Gates"

or facets of God, as we proceed in our Bible interpretations. "And it was so," which completes verse 15,
emphasizes that these Twelve Gates or Most Important
Facets of God are real, and that they work. To the extent
that they are invisible, they are more real, and they work
better than the visible things in the universe. This is
because they are Cause, whereas the things in the visible
universe are Effect. The Apostle Paul said it best when he
said: "Through faith we understand that the worlds were
framed by the word of God, so that things which are seen
were not made of things which do appear;"[3] and: "For the
invisible things of Him, from the creation of the world,
are clearly seen, being understood by the things that are
made."[4] Therefore, these Twelve Gates or Seven Steps
are real, they are invisible, and they are Cause.

[3]Hebrews 11:3
[4]Romans 1:20

*And God made two great lights; the greater light to rule the
day, and the lesser light to rule the night: He made the stars
also.*

GENESIS 1:16

The greater light, of course, refers to the sun,
whereas the lesser light refers to the moon. But
these are literal interpretations that only go so
far. What do the sun and the moon stand for, metaphysically? The sun stands for the absolute Truth about any
thing. The moon represents the intellectual truth only.
For instance, the intellectual, or scientific truth about
man claims that he is a collection of chemicals worth
about ninety nine cents or thereabouts, whereas the
absolute Truth knows that Man is an individualization of
God, who was never born and will never die. This is the
Real Man, God's Man, the Christ within. Our modern
world has glorified the intellectual truth, while over-
looking the absolute Truth. The intellectual truth rules
the night, which means error. So the intellectual truth is
not the truth at all, it is really falsehood. Therefore, it
does not exist.

The stars refer, among other things, to the twelve
signs of the Zodiac. These were important in ancient
astronomy and in Bible astronomy. They correspond to
the Twelve Tribes, the Twelve Gates, and the Twelve
Jewels in the Holy Temple of Revelation.

And God set them in the firmament of the heaven to give light upon the earth.

GENESIS 1:17

T he "stars," in addition to referring to the signs of the Zodiac, also mean the constellations. There are thirty six constellations, with three constellations belonging to each zodiacal sign. If we add the thirty six constellations to the twelve signs of the Zodiac, we have the number forty eight, which is also a mystically significant number of the Bible. For instance, there were forty eight levitical cities in the Bible. If we use the Zodiac to try to predict the future, then we are misusing it, and dabbling in occultism or astrology. But if we use the Zodiac to understand the spiritual significance of the Bible, then we find that it frequently gives us the key, not only to the secret meaning of the Bible, but of ourselves. Indeed, the Bible is really not about times long ago or people long dead. The Bible is not primarily literature or history, though there is a lot of great literature and fascinating history in it. The Bible is about you and me. And unless it can be related to you and me, it means nothing. The Bible is not really a book. It is a spiritual cyclone. It is a spiritual tool to help us to learn about ourselves in the Mind of God.

And to rule over the day and over the night, and to divide the light from the darkness: and God saw that it was good.

GENESIS 1:18

T he greater light to rule the day, which is the sun, means the absolute Truth about anything, as was mentioned earlier. The lesser light to rule the night, which is the moon, means the reflected light or the merely intellectual truth about anything, which is really falsehood. Dividing the light from the darkness is really man's continuing journey in learning to distinguish Truth from error. For the sexaholic, lust or acting out is really the darkness. But when the sexaholic learns to distinguish between lust and that which is not lust, then he is dividing the light from the darkness in his own life. Whenever he uses the laws of mind action to deny the negative, whether it be fear, resentment or self pity or any of the other character defects that may be found in an addict's mind, then he is growing into the image and likeness of the Man God wants him to be. And God sees that it is, indeed, good.

And the evening and the morning were the fourth day.
GENESIS 1:19

The evening, as we previously mentioned, refers to the previous night, and, because it refers to the night, it refers to error. The morning is the only real part of the fourth day. And the fourth day, in the seven numbered stages of Treatment, refers to faith. Faith means substance. Substance is the real reality out of which the world is made. "Faith is the substance of things hoped for."[5] Substance is also Spirit, one of the Seven Most Important Facets of God. Therefore, Faith equals Substance equals Spirit. No wonder Faith can move mountains. Faith works with the very essence of the universe. If you have real Faith (as opposed to belief or hope) there is absolutely nothing that you cannot accomplish. You can restore an arm or raise from the dead. However, if your faith is insufficient, then you had better go to the doctor. That is why some people die who restrict themselves to spiritual means of healing only. They do not rise high enough in consciousness. If you have a serious illness of a life threatening nature, and your healing consciousness has not risen high enough, then you had better pocket your pride and go to the doctor.

---

[5]Hebrews 11:1

And God said, "Let the waters bring forth abundantly the moving creature that hath life, and fowl that may fly above the earth in the open firmament of heaven."

GENESIS 1:20

T he literal aspect of this verse, of course, refers to the evolution of animal and bird species according to the Word of God. It has a deeper meaning, however, that applies directly to us, to you and to me. Every single verse of the Bible refers directly to you and to me, because the Bible is the Supreme Text-book that teaches the human race how to live. It is not a mere book, however. It is a spiritual cyclone. It can transform you and me, if we allow it, into what God wants us to become. It is a spiritual magic carpet. It can transport you and me, if we allow it, wherever God wants us to go. It has been misunderstood and misinterpreted over the ages by priests, ministers, scientists, and others into something that it is not, in order to help prop up religions, belief systems, governments etc... by deceiving the people about its true meaning. That is why it is written in symbols and allegory, so that its true meaning could escape detection until the right time and the right place. During all times and ages there have been gifted people who were able to discover the real meaning of the Bible through inspiration from God. Since the advent of New Thought or the New Age, the number of these people has multiplied, and the diffusion of the real meaning of the Bible has accelerated, so that more and more people are becoming aware of the true meaning of the Bible, and are beginning to use the Bible to transform their lives.

Each verse of the Bible has multiple layers of meaning, like an onion, and it can be interpreted at different levels, according to the readiness of the individual, and the inspiration that he or she receives from God.

Verse twenty is made up of seven parts: 1) "And God said," 2) "Let the waters bring forth abundantly," 3) "the moving creature that hath life," 4) "and fowl that may fly above the earth," 5) "in the open," 6) "firmament," 7) "of heaven." The first part, "and God said," refers to the creation of God's ideas by the universal process of Thought. That is why each one of us is a spark of the great Fire of God, because we also think, just like God. God made us this way, because He loves us. In order to create something we must first Think about it. We must have the idea before we can proceed to the plan and take action on the plan. The idea is sometimes referred to as "the Word" in the Bible. Nothing can be created, nothing can happen without the Word. It is sometimes called the "Creative Word," because its function is to create in the realm of thought that which is to appear in the realm of manifestation. We use the same process of creation that God uses, in the realm of our world, only it is on a much smaller scale, because it involves usually only us, the people we know, the people we think about, our health, and our circumstances etc... "And God said" refers to one of the Seven Most Important Facets of God called Principle. Principle refers to the Law of Cause and Effect, both in the visible and invisible world. For instance, in the visible world, there is a law of physics called gravity, and it refers to the mutual attraction of physical bodies. For example, if I am dropped from an airplane without a parachute, then the chances are that my body will be attracted to the body of the earth, and start plummeting down faster and faster until it crashes. It does not matter if I am a famous person, or an important person, or just "Joe Blow." We will all equally plummet to the earth and crash and probably go through the experience called death. It does not matter if we are living according to the will of God or not, we will probably equally go through the experience called death. God does not make an exception to the Law of Principle because an important person fell out of the airplane. Now in the invisible world, the Law of Cause and Effect usually works something like this: People end up getting what they deserve in this world or the next. It is sometimes phrased, "What goes around comes around." Emerson wrote a beautiful essay on Compensation, and I will refer the reader to it for a fuller explanation of the concept. It is the opposite of the concept, "Why bad things sometimes happen to good people," prevalent in our modern secular age, which sometimes tries to deny the Law of Compensation. Another Principle of Spiritual Law is "Like attracts like," and so forth. So the long and short of it is, regarding "God said," is that, just as God must have an Idea before it beomes manifestation, so must we. We must think of something before it can become manifest in our world. In other words, we must "say the word." This is an expression or concept frequently found in the Bible, both the Old and New Testaments. "Ask and ye shall receive" is another form of this. If we continually think of negative things, then negative things will happen to us, because we have "said the word." If we think of beautiful, high-minded things, then, sooner or later, good things will start happening to us.

The second part of this verse reads, "Let the waters bring forth abundantly." Waters, in this sense, refer to Spirit or Substance out of which all things are made. Now we said earlier that Substance meant Faith, as in "Now faith is the substance of things hoped for,"[6] and indeed it does. Ideas do not become manifest in our world unless we believe that they will and are grateful for that fact ahead of time. So Faith and Substance are inextricably intertwined. One cannot work for us without the other. So "the waters" bringing "forth abundantly" refers to the process of creation, which takes place from the Sea of undifferentiated universal Substance to the Land of specific manifestation through the agency of the Word. And the inspired writer tells us that this process takes place "abundantly". God does not work in a chintzy or niggardly manner. He works abundantly. The Laws of God also work abundantly. When we use the Laws of God, according to His will, they work abundantly.

"The moving creature that hath life" refers to Thought itself. Rene Descartes, the famous French philosopher and mathematician, once said, "I think, therefore I am." One cannot think if one does not exist. We do not stop thinking just because we make our transition from the earth plane to the next plane of existence. But if we were to stop existing (which is an impossibility), then we

[6]Hebrews 11:1

would stop thinking, because thinking is a characteristic of Life. It is also a characteristic of Intelligence, which is another Most important Facet of God, which will be discussed in the next part of this twentieth verse. Now the "moving creature that hath life," on a superficial level, refers to animal life, and one of the features that is most characteristic of animals is Life. Take a newborn puppy, wagging his tail furiously, full of the joy of living. When we express the joy of living, we are glorifying God, and expressing true happiness. Life is one of the Seven Most Important Facets of God. When we use our gift of Life to think happy thoughts, then we will surely demonstrate good in our lives. This means purging character defects from our thoughts. For the sexaholic this means elimination of fear, resentment, and lust from his or her thoughts. This can be accomplished through prayer and meditation, as well as the practice of the Twelve Steps of recovery. Other character defects of mine include self-pity, expectations, excessive dependence upon others, sentiment, criticism, jealousy, envy, over-sensitiveness, eagerness to be praised, cowardice about being blamed, penury (consciousness of poverty rather than abundance), being glad that my enemies are unfortunate, discouragement when I do not succeed, loneliness (different from being alone), pride, impatience, gluttony, sloth, ingratitude, and these are just the first twenty of the first eighty five identified so far, and there are probably more. More will be listed later. So, in order to express the joy of living, it is necessary to humbly ask God to remove the character defects I have accumulated during my life of addiction to alcohol and lust which express death, rather than Life. Little animals, such as puppies, not only express Life, but also Intelligence, and Spirit (All is Spirit). However, they probably do not possess Souls in the sense of being individualizations of God, who were <u>individually</u> never born and will <u>individually</u> never die.

"And fowl that may fly above the earth" refers to thoughts that soar, because they are inspired by God—in other words, God-like thoughts. Fowl have wings, and wings symbolize independence from physical handicaps, so they fly above the earth-bound. Where "the moving creature that hath life" symbolizes thoughts generically, fowl, because they can fly, represent thoughts that fly upward or God-ward. In other words, spiritual thoughts. We get these spiritual thoughts from practicing prayer and meditation. These thoughts are necessary for us, as sexaholics, if we are to have victory over lust and acting out. They are as necessary to us as air is to the health of the physical body. Deprived of air, the body dies. Deprived of prayer and meditation and spiritual thoughts, the Soul dies, and the body also soon after.

The next part of Verse Twenty has one word, "open." It is an adjective that modifies "firmament." Now firmament, we learned earlier, means faith and understanding about the Truth. So the "open firmament" really means unlimited faith and understanding about the Truth. This is what we will achieve as a result of prayer and meditation, and this, in turn will result in Demonstration of the "big five" miracles: Happiness, Harmony, Health, Success, and Prosperity, of which we will speak more later.

We have now discussed parts five and six of Verse Twenty. There is only one remaining part: Heaven. Now heaven does not mean pie-in-the-sky or a future happiness somewhere else. Heaven means right here and right now. It is the awareness of being in agreement with the thoughts of the Christ Within. It is the realization that I am in eternity **NOW**. It is the realization, in the midst of chaos and seeming turmoil, in tribulation: "I can hardly wait to see the Good that's going to come out of this." It is the realization that seeming evil does not exist in Truth, that evil is but an illusion.

*And God created great whales, and every living creature
that moveth, which the waters brought forth abundantly,
after their kind, and every winged fowl after his kind: and
God saw that it was good.*

GENESIS 1:21

 hale really means sea-creature, and "creature"
comes from the Hebrew word *nephesh*, which
is used 754 times in the Old Testament, but is
translated in different ways in different places in the
Bible. Now "creature," according to Webster, means
"something created." In order to be created, a creature
needs to be thought about by God, as we learned in the
previous verses of Genesis, and man, made in the image
and likeness of God, partakes of this ability to create
also. Therefore, a creature needs a thought in back of it
in order to exist. The New Thought movement teaches
that thoughts are things, and, indeed, they are, but things
are also thoughts. Things have to have a thought in back
of them in order to exist. Things do not exist unless they
are thought about. So we can say that creatures <u>are</u>
thoughts. And the thought that they (the creatures) represent varies with the type of creature. Now some trans-
lators of the Bible have used the word "monsters of the
deep" to mean Great sea-creature, instead of the word
"whale", but this is incorrect because it implies that God
would create something monstrous or evil. God is incapable of creating anything evil because he is too pure to
behold evil or create it. God cannot do or create anything
but Good. The evil that is in this world is strictly as a
result of man's "many inventions". Man has free will,

and was created to be able to choose wrongly, or to choose error, if he wished to. The only way that man can grow into the image and likeness of God is to <u>voluntarily</u> choose the Good, instead of error. That is one of the main differences between God and man: God cannot voluntarily choose error, but man can. The monsters of the deep really represent man's own error thoughts. They have nothing in common with the peaceful, happy whales of God.

"Every living creature that moveth," then, symbolizes all the different thoughts of God, and "which the waters brought forth abundantly" refers to the Universal Sea of Mind or Substance, out of which was created "every living creature" by the action of God's Word. "After their kind," of course, refers to the kind of thought involved. "And every winged fowl after his kind," as was noted earlier, refers to thoughts of a more spiritual nature, because they are liberated from more earth-bound limitations. "And God saw that it was good" means God admiring His own handiwork and reinforcing the concept that we just introduced: God is incapable of doing or thinking anything that is not Good. Whenever the Bible alludes to God or the Lord in connection with anything that is not Good, it is usually associated with a man (or woman—we are, of course, using "man" in the generic sense), and it is the man, who, by making the wrong decision, substitutes <u>his own understanding</u> for God's, and proceeds to think error thoughts or perform error acts, sometimes without realizing what is happening. For instance, in Exodus, when it says that the Lord hardened Pharaoh's heart, it was not the Lord at all, but Pharaoh's own mistaken perception of the Lord that hardened his heart. God does not harden people's hearts. He gives them the freedom to make their own mistakes.

And God blessed them, saying, "Be fruitful, and multiply, and fill the waters in the seas, and let fowl multiply in the earth."

GENESIS 1:22

T o bless something or someone means to wish that thing or person well. And God, by His very nature, is incapable of doing anything else. When we forgive someone who has injured us and wish him or her well, we are acting in a God-like way. As a matter of fact the very act of forgiveness blesses us and enriches us.

When God tells the creatures of the sea, and the fowl to "be fruitful and multiply" He is, in reality, communicating His own Good thoughts to fecundate and multiply themselves or each other. That is why fish, in metaphysics, symbolize proliferation and productivity. And fruitfulness, in metaphysics, symbolizes the opulent consciousness man and woman develop as a result of lofty perceptions of Truth.

And the evening and the morning were the fifth day.
GENESIS 1:23

The fifth Gate of the Heavenly Jerusalem is Works, or manifestation or demonstration. It is the result of mental Treatment. When God created the fish and the fowl, it was as a result of His having thought about them. When we create prosperous or happy circumstances in our lives at home or at work, it is always as a result of thinking Good, positive thoughts first. We reap what we sow. This is the Law of Cause and Effect, and it is very Good.

And God said, "Let the earth bring forth the living creature
after his kind, cattle, and creeping thing, and beast of the
earth after his kind:" and it was so.

GENESIS 1:24

T he sixth Gate of the Heavenly Jerusalem stands
for Understanding. This has a different meaning from the Understanding associated with
Denial, which is the second Gate. The sixth Gate Understanding means understanding of how the Almighty
works. We understand the secret of Demonstration. It is
a summary of the entire thinking faculty, which is what
makes us like God, because we are created in His image
and likeness. All of a sudden, we understand how the first
five Gates work: 1) The name of God, which gives us
Life; 2) Denial of the not-God, which gives us health; 3)
Affirmation of All as Good, which gives us strength; 4)
Faith, which gives us support; and 5) Works, which gives
us the manifestation or Demonstration of our prayer or
Treatment. So, as a result of our Understanding, the
Demonstration continues. When the inspired writer states,
"And God said," he means, of course, that God is using
His creative Word to bring forth something that He is
thinking, and the expression "Let the earth bring forth"
does not mean to allow or permit the earth, which
symbolizes manifestation or Demonstration, but means,
more directly that manifestation is actually bringing
forth. In other words "Let" is a figure of speech meaning
that whoever is being "let" is actually doing it. So the
phrase could be re-worded to say, "The earth is bringing

forth," because all that is needed is for God to speak the Word, and the manifestation is a certainty. And what is manifestation bringing forth? The living creature. And what is meant by the living creature? Living, of course, refers to Life, which is one of the Seven Most Important Facets of God. And creature, as we discovered earlier, symbolizes a thought. So the earth is bringing forth living thoughts in the form of cattle and creeping things and beasts of the earth. Cattle are thoughts involving physical sense and toughness. Creeping things are thoughts that symbolize physical pleasure. Beasts of the earth signify material thoughts generally. Now physical sensation, toughness, physical pleasure, and material thoughts are not in themselves erroneous, if they form part of a valid spiritual act. For instance, it is necessary to utilize physical sensation, which is mediated through the five senses of sight, taste, smell, touch, and hearing, in order to function in the world. So physical sense or sensation when used as part of doing God's will for me today is good and even "very good," because God gave us ears, a sense of touch, a sense of smell, eyes to see, and a tongue to taste. He endowed us with these senses, because he meant us to use them. When we use them as part of His plan, we are glorifying Him. There is nothing wrong with being physically tough, because that is a gift from God that helps us get through life. If we are a boxer or a football player, we need to be physically tough in order to succeed. There is nothing wrong with physical pleasure when it is used in harmony with God's will. There is nothing wrong with the enjoyment of good food or drink. There is nothing wrong with the pleasure of orgasm if we are having sex with our spouse, so long as lust or excessive dependency are not mixed in with it. There is nothing wrong with material thoughts about a house if an architect is going to draw up plans for it. As a matter of fact, these material thoughts, about capitals, lintels, crossbeams, walls, bricks etc... are necessary if the architect is going to be able to build the house. Similarly, if a physician is going to treat a patient, it is necessary for him or her to do a good history, physical exam, and order laboratory tests. And these all require material thoughts to be accomplished. But, when these physical sensations become detached from their God given purpose, their "spiritual component," if you will, then they may acquire a "life" of their own and become addictive, and existing for their own sake, apart from God, lead to sin, sickness, and death. If, instead of using these material senses as part of a means to an end of doing God's will for us today, we use them selfishly, for our own secret pleasure, they become an end in themselves, and we begin to worship them, as the ancients worshiped idols, and we practice idolatry. That is what idolatry is. Idolatry is the preoccupation with anything apart from God. The worship of the creature instead of the Creator, the effect instead of the Cause.

"After his kind," which is repeated twice in verse 24, means "of every sort," which, interpreted spiritually, means that these various material thoughts and physical pleasures run an infinite gamut, just as human beings present an infinite variety. Each one of us is unique, even identical twins differ in subtle ways. Some like to play tennis, others like to ski. Some like to crochet and others like to sew. Some sports fans like soccer, others like football, still others basketball, and still others baseball, ice hockey, or cricket. Some people like to read, some like to watch television, others like to go to the movies or collect videos of movies. Similarly, when it comes to the perversion of these God given pleasures, there are infinite varieties: Some are overeaters, others drug addicts, still others alcoholics, and still others sexaholics. And among the sexaholics themselves, there are many different varieties or "drugs of choice." For instance, some lust addicts are turned on by prostitutes, others by masturbation, still others by pornography. Some are exhibitionists, some sadists, and others masochists. Some prey on children, some on animals, others on dead bodies. Some are heterosexual, others homosexual, and still others bisexual. Some like to have a repetitive and endless series of romances. Others just want to rape or kill. These perversions were not created by God, they are the result of man's "many inventions," his error choices. And since they are erroneous indeed, they do not exist in Truth. They only possess the "life" given to them by the ignorance and stupidity of the unfortunate human beings who pursue them. Like the viruses that can only exist inside a human body, they would disappear without a host to entertain and nurture them.

"And it was so." This is a repetition of previous, similar or identical phrases. All these things are so, because we live in God's world, and there are no accidents or mistakes. Everything that happens happens because it's supposed to happen. It happens because of Law or Principle, or the Law of Cause and Effect. If we want to achieve Happiness, Harmony, Health, Success, and Prosperity, then we must use the Law to our benefit and stop fighting it. We must humbly ask God to take away the error and give us only Truth.

*And God made the beast of the earth after his kind, and cattle
after their kind, and every thing that creepeth upon the earth
after his kind: and God saw that it was good.*

GENESIS 1:25

s we noted in the 24th verse, the beast of
the earth symbolizes ideas of God involving
material thoughts generally; cattle, thoughts
of physical sense and toughness; "and every thing that
creepeth upon the earth" symbolizes physical pleasure.
And we also noted that these things were all Good in
themselves, especially when used in conjuction with
God's will, and only fell into the realm of error when man
or woman used his or her own God-given free will to
misuse them. When a man or woman, for instance, uses
his or her free will to spend most of his or her time on the
pursuit of wealth for its own sake, or the amassing of real
estate, or buying up corporations, or scientific investiga-
tion, or the writing of articles and books on scholarly or
worldly subjects, or becomes a "workaholic" by becoming so obsessed with his or her occupation that he or she
becomes a slave to it, then that man or woman becomes
an idolator, because he or she worships the created thing
instead of the Creator. The same thing happens to the
addict, whether the addiction is to food, drugs, alcohol,
gambling, stealing, or lust, except that addiction is
generally held in lower esteem by the public than being
obsessed with money or worldly subjects. These latter
are considered respectable obsessions, because they are
not usually illegal. Most addictions, on the other hand,

are so obviously harmful to the individual and to society, that they carry the burden of heavy societal disapproval. But in point of fact, they are not so different one from the other. Both are characterized by leaving God out. In this book of Bible interpretation, we are focusing on meta-physics and on addiction to lust. And we have discovered that the best way to recover from sexaholism is to turn to God. We do not really have a solution for people who are not addicted to a specific addiction, but who are scien-tists without religious convictions, for example, or secu-lar humanists who deny that God exists, or just plain "workaholics." They too have to find their own answers in the crucible of their own lives. In some cases, they, too (just like the addict) will "hit bottom", and, out of the desperation of their predicament, will find a Higher Power that works for them. There have been many cases of religious conversions of persons who smugly or comfortably thought that they could contentedly coast through life without grappling with the issue of God in their lives, until they found that things were just not working out for them anymore. In desperation (like the proverbial person in the fox-hole who finds that he or she is no longer an atheist) they asked for God's help or made some type of statement, such as, "God, if you exist, will you help me now?" And these people are frequently, seemingly miraculously, helped. But this book is not really for the purpose of helping these "normies," as we call them in AA. They are welcome to read it, they are welcome to derive any benefit they may from this book, but this book is not really addressed to them.

The last phrase in verse twenty-five, "and God saw that it was good" again emphasizes the fact that these material thoughts or ideas come from God, and only become errors when misused by man utilizing his free will. The eastern style of writing makes use of repetition a lot. We need repetition in order to learn. Repetition is good for us.

And God said, "let Us make man in Our image, after Our likeness: and let them have dominion over the fish of the sea, and over the fowl of the air, and over the cattle, and over all the earth, and over every creeping thing that creepeth upon the earth."

GENESIS 1:26

N ow this verse states that man was created in the image and likeness of God, in the very beginning, even before there was a man upon the earth (man does not physically appear in the Bible account until verse seven of chapter two). The man in verse 26 is "ideal man." He was the man that was created from the very beginning in the mind of God: "According as he hath chosen us in him before the foundation of the world."[7] You and I were never born, and you and I will never die. You and I have been carried, as individuals, in the mind of God, from the very beginning. And since God is eternal, there has never been a "beginning" per se. So we have always existed, and will never cease to exist, as we go from glory to glory. So it is not so strange, then, since we are such glorious creatures in reality, that God would have given us dominion over the fish of the sea (symbolizing all thoughts generally) and over the fowl of the air (symbolizing spiritually elevated thoughts) and over the cattle (symbolizing material thoughts of sensation and strength), over all the earth (symbolizing all manifestation), and over every creeping thing that

[7]Ephesians 1:4

creepeth upon the earth (symbolizing thoughts of material pleasure). The reality of our glorious selves is that we have **DOMINION**. And this dominion is granted to us through the power of our own thoughts. That is why it is so important to carefully guard our thought life. "Keep thy heart with all diligence, for out of it are the issues of life."[8]

---

[8]Proverbs 4:23

So God created man in His own image, in the image of God created He him; male and female created He them.

GENESIS 1:27

his is one of the most important verses in the whole Bible, because it introduces the concept of the male and female principles. Now we are all made of varying admixtures of male and female principles, regardless of our sex. And God did not create us from the beginning of time (which of course never began) as little men or little women. He created the male and female principles of Life. We as individuals have probably incarnated in different times as members of both sexes. And whether we are a man or a woman at present is probably not very important. Our mental and spiritual qualities are much more crucial, and do not necessarily depend on our gender. Now the masculine Principle involves intellect, whereas the feminine involves intuition. Law is masculine, whereas Love is feminine. Understanding is masculine, and Wisdom is feminine. In general, feeling is feminine and knowledge is masculine. Now, in order to be a complete person in the image and likeness of God, we need both. In order to have a successful Demonstration in metaphysics, we also need both. That is why the Fifth Commandment reads: "Honour thy father and thy mother: that thy days may be long upon the land which the LORD thy God giveth thee."[9] Father is masculine and mother is femi-

---

[9]Exodus 20:12

nine. Father stands for the knowledge of what we want to demonstrate, and mother stands for the feeling that the demonstration will be successful. This feeling can be described as unassailable Faith and Gratitude for the accomplished Demonstration ahead-of-time. Knowledge without feeling is insufficient. It is necessary to have polarity. In order to have a successful Demonstration it is necessary to have polarity. Polarity is defined by Webster as, "The possession or manifestation of two opposing attributes, tendencies, or principles." Knowledge without feeling will not do it, and feeling without knowledge will not either. We have to have both. And to be a complete, successful human being we have to have both also. As we grow into the ideal Man created by God, we will have both Principles within ourselves, and when we make our transition to the next plane of existence, we will no longer manifest the characteristics of our gender on earth during this incarnation. Spirit is without gender.

And God blessed them, and God said unto them, "Be fruitful, and multiply, and replenish the earth, and subdue it: and have dominion over the fish of the sea, and over the fowl of the air, and over every living thing that moveth upon the earth."

GENESIS 1:28

"T hem," of course, refers to Adam and Eve, of which we will hear more later. In this verse, the Bible is emphasizing that man (generic man, which includes man and woman) is to have **DOMINION** over his thoughts: First, his thoughts will be "fruitful," productive of much fruition, manifestation, and Demonstration of all kinds; his thoughts will "multiply," which means that his thoughts will be productive of other thoughts, which will also, in turn produce their own fruition, manifestation, and Demonstrations of all kinds. These manifestations will "replenish the earth, and subdue it." And to make sure that there is no misunderstanding on this score, the inspired writer repeats this theme using different words: Man is to have "dominion" over all ideas of proliferation and fruitfulness (for that is what fish symbolize metaphysically); man is to have "dominion" over all spiritual or elevated thoughts (for that is what fowl symbolize when they fly); and, finally man is to have "dominion" over all the practical, concrete, and scientific thoughts—the thoughts that enable man and woman to do things in a material world (for that is what other living things that move upon the face of the earth symbolize). And we must not forget the very first four words of this verse: "And God blessed them." When a man or woman blesses somebody, it generally means that he or she is wishing that person well: Wishing that person the "Big Five"—i.e., Happiness, Harmony, Health, Success, and Prosperity. When one wishes somebody those five things honestly and with true sincerity, it is impossible to harbor resentments or anger against that person. But when God blesses somebody, what does that mean? When God blesses somebody, since He Himself is the source and substance of that which He is wishing, then all these things automatically become true, right here and right now on the etheric plane, and probably fairly soon on the plane of manifestation, which is the so-called earth plane. And if you and I use the laws of scientific Christianity, which means that we use the same laws that God uses, and if we rise high enough in consciousness while we are treating, then the same thing will happen when we bless somebody, and we will be blessed also in return. That is why Love is the fulfillment of the Law. There is nothing that Love cannot accomplish. And if we use Love to accomplish it, in order to help someone else, then we will be helped ourselves one hundred-fold.

Now when it says in the Bible verse that God blessed them, meaning Adam and Eve, it does not mean that there were two real, historical personages by the name of Adam and Eve. I do not believe that Adam and Eve were real people. They are symbols. Adam symbolizes the masculine pole of existence and Eve, the feminine. The masculine pole of existence stands for the intellectual or knowledge aspect of reality. Two of the Seven Most Important Facets of God, Truth and Intelligence, belong to the masculine pole. The feminine pole stands for the feeling aspect of reality. Another two of the Seven Most

Important Facets of God, Life and Love, belong to the feminine pole. Now for any Demonstration to take effect, as was previously mentioned, the masculine and feminine poles must both be in place and working: i.e., the knowledge and the feeling, or the Father and the Mother. The two columns at the entrance of the Temple of Solomon, Jachin and Boaz, also stand for these two poles. Law is sometimes referred to as the Divine Masculine, and Love, the Divine Feminine. Wisdom is frequently considered feminine in the Bible, and Understanding, masculine. Now Wisdom is a compound attribute made up of both Love and Intelligence, and Understanding is another compound attribute made up of Truth and Intelligence, so that Wisdom would be mostly feminine and part masculine and Understanding mostly masculine.

And God said, "Behold, I have given you every herb bearing seed, which is upon the face of all the earth, and every tree, in the which is the fruit of a tree yielding seed; to you it shall be for meat."

GENESIS 1:29

N ow "behold" is an old-fashioned term that means "Look!" In the days when the King James Version was written, "behold" was the current word, but nowadays we would say "Look!" or "See!" Herb, of course, means plant. So on a literal level, the Bible is telling us that God said, "Look! I have given you every plant that bears seed, which is upon the face of all the earth, and every tree, in which is fruit, which also bears seed; and you can eat the fruit." Does this mean that man was supposed to be a vegetarian? Here we go again getting literal. If we get too literal, we will miss the whole spiritual meaning of the Bible. I do not mean to criticize either meat-eaters or vegetarians. That is not the point. The Bible is about much more than diet, important as that may be. Remember the Bible means, "This means **ME**." What do plants, seeds, earth, trees, fruit, and food have to do with me? What do these terms mean spiritually or symbolically? What is the true meaning of this seemingly obscure verse of the Bible?

In general terms, this verse talks about fruits and vegetables. Now ancient man, before he became a hunter, was a gatherer of fruits, plants, and vegetables, growing in the wild. These things were his source of food and sustenance. Food and sustenance symbolize everything that we need in this life in order to achieve our goal:

Money, parents, friends, teachers, connections, jobs, etc... So fruits, plants, and vegetables, on one level, represent that which we need in order to survive and prosper. But God is telling us particularly to eat fruit, because it contains seed. Now, metaphysically, seed means "The Word of God". So this verse is really telling us, in unmistakeable terms, that in order to get the things that we need in order to make our Demonstration, we must nourish ourselves spiritually with the Word of God. It is more important to pray and meditate than it is to work in the material plane of existence towards a goal. Not that God does not expect or want us to do the footwork. He does. But without the prayer and meditation we will lack the inspiration, the master plan, the idea of what it is that we want to do. We will lack the knowledge of the goal we must aspire to. All the footwork, or sweat and strain in the world is worthless if we know not what we seek. We can spend hours and days and weeks working in the <u>wrong direction</u>. The man or woman who allows his or her life to be guided by God in all things great or small will automatically be the right person in the right place at the right time, seemingly without effort. Helpful, time-saving shortcuts will appear like magic. That is why all persons engaged in Truth work learn to spend at least one half hour or one hour or more in prayer and meditation daily, preferrably in the morning. They read at least seven verses of the Bible daily, savoring them slowly and extracting the spiritual meat. Then they meditate on what they have read. And meditation is not some arcane, obscure skill. It only means concentrated thinking about God. It does not require assuming any particular position of the body, only the concentration of the mind and Spirit. Any one can learn to do it. If we do it, we will find that it transforms our entire life.

ow, as previously mentioned, "every beast of the earth" symbolizes practical thoughts, "fowl of the air" symbolizes spiritual thoughts, "every thing that creepeth upon the earth" symbolizes sensate or earth-bound thoughts. Now, thoughts are things, and things are thoughts, and thoughts are, in a sense, alive, because they can only be conceptualized by an entity that is alive, and the inspired writer tells us that there is Life in these thoughts, as well as in the animals that represent them: "Wherein there is life." Now to each of these thoughts, and to the animals that symbolize them, He has given "every green herb for meat." This means that He is giving nourishment or sustenance to these thoughts, so that they will go forth and demonstrate in the world of manifestation, and not return empty-handed. So every thought is sent out for the purpose of changing things. Therefore, every thought is a prayer, as prayer is also for the purpose of changing things. Everything we think is, therefore, a prayer, for either good or ill, and, since evil does not exist in Truth, we call "ill" "error." Error thoughts lead to sin, sickness, and death, and good thoughts lead to Happiness, Harmony, Health, Success, and Prosperity, but all thoughts lead to somewhere. As individualizations of God, we have been given free will, which means freedom to think what thoughts we wish. But once our thoughts are sent, they are like a missile, bearing with them their own physics and mathematics, and cannot be called back. One of the Seven Most Important Facets of God called Principle sends the missiles hurtling on to their destination, and they will, inevitably cause an effect or manifestation. Therefore, it behooves us to guard our thoughts. "Keep thy heart with all diligence, for out of it are the issues of life."[10]

The verse ends with the phrase, "And it was so." This is an expression with a double meaning in this context. On the one hand, it is so, when God has said it, because the Word of God never fails to demonstrate. On the other hand, it is also so, when man, utilizing his own, God-given free will, thinks a thought, whether Truth or error, because it too will have its own demonstration, whether for good or ill, as we said before.

---

[10]Proverbs 4:23

And God saw every thing that He had made, and behold, it was very good. And the evening and the morning were the sixth day.

GENESIS 1:31

The sixth day corresponds to the stage of metaphysical treatment or prayer, which is Release, which means to stop working mentally on the problem, and just contemplate our own enjoyment of what has taken place, or what we believe will shortly take place. "And God saw every thing that He had made, and behold, it was very good." This is the keynote of the entire Bible: All is Good. Apparent evil and inharmony are not real, because there is nothing but Good. As we continue to grow and change into the image and likeness of God, we forget the seemingly unpleasant things that seem to dog our footsteps during our daily travails, just as a child forgets the thing that made him or her cry yesterday. We are going to live forever, so nothing can really harm us. If we are sexaholic and are trying to live without lust, one day at a time, or one hour at a time, then we are doing God's will right here and right now, and nothing "bad" can befall us. He will take care of us now and in the beyond, and, more than that, will surely grant us a great Demonstration. All we have to do is to be patient, grin and bear it, and any seeming evil will all turn out for the best, because God turns everything into Good.

In tribulation, glory...
Glory in tribulation...
And state: I praise the Lord!—I
praise the Lord!—I praise the Lord!
And miraculously Good and
greater Good begin pouring forth!